Abomination of Desolation

Arlin E. Nusbaum

Abomination of Desolation

Arlin E. Nusbaum

Alpha and Omega Publishing (2013)

ISBN 978-1-60135-278-1

Table of Contents

Introduction

This is part two of a three part series on *The Revelation of John*. The premise to the series as stated in Vol. I is this: If *The Revelation of John* was only for our time, why was it given nearly two thousand years ago? Another way of stating the position is this: If it is only about end time events, and if those events have not yet happened, why was it given nearly two thousand years ago? Surely it has relevance not only for our time, but also for those who lived two thousand years ago and everyone in-between. That is the premise to the three part series.

Part I was about the first and last three chapters of *The Revelation of John* and was titled *The Alpha & The Omega, The Beginning and The Ending of The Revelation of John*. In that volume we learned that *The Revelation of John* is more than a book of prophecy, that in fact, it is a handbook for Christian living and a blueprint for how believers will be judged. *The Alpha* part contains teachings, admonitions, and promises that are mostly overlooked by readers who go to *The Revelation of John* to learn just about prophecies. That is unfortunate. *The Omega* contains rewards for those faithful to *The Alpha*.

Although a book of prophecy, Vol. I demonstrated one reason why *The Revelation of John* has been pertinent for two thousand years. Another reason *The Revelation of John* was given two thousand years ago is found in the current volume, Vol. II, *The Abomination of Desolation. The Revelation of John* is about "things which are, and the things which shall be hereafter." (Rev. 1:19) Part of the confusion about *The Revelation of John* comes from prophecy writers interpreting the "things which are" as "things which shall be hereafter." After examining the prophecies in *The Revelation of John* and other books of prophecy I have discovered that the prophecy of *The Abomination of Desolation* is at the core of most misunderstandings.

Two Camps

I learned that there are two competing camps of thought regarding *The Abomination of Desolation.* One that says it's already here and the other that says it has not yet come. Those who believe it has already come may refer to themselves as *Historicists* and those who believe it will yet come as *Futurists.* Popular prophecy writers such as Tim Lahaye of *Left Behind* fame, John Hagee, Hal Lindsey, Grant Jeffrey, Jack Van Impe, Perry Stone, Paul Crouch, etc. are all in the camp that believes it will yet come. Steve Wohlberg of *The Left Behind Deception* and early Bible commentators are in the other camp.

Misunderstandings

The misunderstanding of **fulfilled prophecy** begins with the *Abomination of Desolation* (Daniel 9:24-27) and ends with the *Man of Sin* prophecy (2 Thessalonians 2:3-4). Prophecy writers have jumped to some conclusions as to who the antichrist is by wrongly joining those two prophecies. Here they are:

Daniel 9:24-27

> 24 **Seventy weeks are determined** upon thy people and upon thy holy city, to finish the transgression, and to make an end of sins, and to make reconciliation for iniquity, and to bring in everlasting righteousness, and to seal up the vision and prophecy, and to anoint the most Holy.
> 25 Know therefore and understand, that from the going forth of the commandment to restore and to build Jerusalem unto the Messiah the Prince shall be seven weeks, and threescore and two weeks: the street shall be built again, and the wall, even in troublous times.
> 26 And after threescore and two weeks shall Messiah be cut off, but not for himself: and the people of the prince that shall come shall destroy the city and the sanctuary; and the end thereof shall be with a flood, and unto the end of the war desolations are determined.
> 27 And **he shall confirm the covenant** with

many for **one week**: and **in the midst of the week he shall cause the sacrifice and the oblation to cease**, and for the **overspreading of abominations he shall make it desolate**, even until the consummation, and that determined shall be poured upon the desolate. (Daniel 9)

2 Thessalonians 2

3 Let no man deceive you by any means: for that
day shall not come, except there come a falling
away first, and that **man of sin be revealed, the
son of perdition;**
4 Who opposeth and exalteth himself above all that
is called God, or that is worshipped; **so that he as
God sitteth in the temple of God, shewing
himself that he is God.** (2 Thessalonians 2)

Early Bible commentators were in agreement that the prophecy in Daniel was about *Jesus* fulfilling the Old Testament covenant, not the antichrist. It has only been in modern times that this view has changed and been replaced by the idea that it pertains to a future antichrist. Regardless, there are some difficulties in conjoining those two prophecies. For one, the word "temple" as used by Paul in 2 Thessalonians 2 does not apply to old covenant, Old Testament temples. A quick review of Paul's temple references will clear this up.

Temples

The apostle Paul was the author of the *Man of Sin* prophecy in 2 Thessalonians 2:3-4. The word "temple" used here by Paul is different from temples of the Old Testament. Here are all the temple references used by Paul:

Your Body A Temple

16 Know ye not that **ye are the temple of God**, and that the Spirit of God dwelleth in you?
17 If any man defile the temple of God, him shall God destroy; for the temple of God is holy, **which temple ye are**. (1 Corinthians 3)

19 What? know ye not that **your body is the temple** of the Holy Ghost which is in you, which ye have of God, and ye are not your own? (1 Corinthians 6)

16 And what agreement hath the temple of God with idols? for **ye are the temple of the living God**; as God hath said, **I will dwell in them**, and **walk in them**; and I will be their God, and they shall be my people. (2 Corinthians 6)

Body of Believers a Temple

18 For through him we both have access by one Spirit unto the Father.
19 Now therefore ye are no more strangers and foreigners, but fellowcitizens with the **saints**, and of the household of God;
20 And are built upon the foundation of the apostles and prophets, Jesus Christ himself being

the chief corner stone;
21 In whom all the building fitly framed together
groweth unto **an holy temple** in the Lord:
22 In whom ye also are builded together for an
habitation of God through the Spirit. (Ephesians 2)

To sum up Paul's view of New Testament temples, they are our bodies and the body of Christ, i.e. The Church. Jesus told us what the fate of the last Old Covenant, Old Testament temple would be in his prophecy found in Matthew 24. I shall review his prophecy next.

Destruction Of The Temple

One day the disciples were bragging to Jesus about how beautiful the buildings of the temple were, whereupon Jesus replied they would all be destroyed:

1 And Jesus went out, and departed from the
temple: and his disciples came to him for to shew
him the **buildings of the temple.**
2 And Jesus said unto them, See ye not all these
things? Verily I say unto you, **There shall not be
left here one stone upon another, that shall not
be thrown down.**
15 When ye therefore shall see the **abomination
of desolation, spoken of by Daniel the
prophet**, stand in the holy place. (Matthew 24)

This destruction was fulfilled in 70 A.D by Titus and is known as the *Siege of Jerusalem* which was

commemorated by the *Arch of Titus* (and other structures):

Roman Jews and the Arch of Titus

"At the southeastern end of the Roman Forum stands a monument whose history resonates into the present: the Arch of Titus. Built around 80 C.E. by the emperor Domitian to honor the victories of his brother Titus and their father Vespasian in the war against Judaea a decade earlier, it served as the Forum's eastern entrance and exit. Its exterior is nearly all a nineteenth-century reconstruction, and the inscription on the side facing the Forum records the restoration of the arch by Pope Pius VII. Although smaller and simpler than the Arch of

Septimius Severus at the Forum's opposite end, it records an event that reverberates to the present day. The Romans' victory in their long and savage war against Judaea put an end to the Jewish state for nearly nineteen hundred years. Only with the foundation of modern Israel in 1948 was the result of Rome's triumph finally undone.

On the walls of the single-arched opening are two sculptured panels celebrating Titus and Vespasian's victory, during which Jerusalem was looted and nearly destroyed. One panel shows Titus riding in a chariot, with the goddess Roma guiding his horses, while the jubilant citizens of Rome crowd around him. On the opposite side we see the start of the triumphal procession that would in fact have passed this way. Soldiers carry the spoils of war, including the **altar table, silver trumpets, and the huge, seven-branched gold candelabrum plundered from the Hebrew temple in Jerusalem**.

Among the other spoils of the Jewish War were thousands of captives. Many were put to work as slaves during the Coliseum's construction, and some may also have worked on the Arch of Titus a decade later-with what bitterness of heart we may easily imagine. The arch became a potent symbol of Jewish defeat, a place the Jews of Rome avoided for centuries, refusing to walk under it.

But on May 14, 1948, the day the State of Israel was founded, all of that changed. As radios announced the rebirth of their ancient homeland, the Jews of Rome, some of them descendants of Titus's captives, spontaneously began pouring in from all over the city and converging on the Arch of Titus. Laughing, shouting, weeping, cheering, banging on metal pots or anything that would make a joyful noise, they skipped, ran, walked, hobbled, or had themselves carried through the Arch of Titus. Today, the immediate surrounding area is closed off and nobody is allowed to walk under it, but Israeli tourists still take each other's pictures in front of this place where history has turned a page." (Judith Testa, Professor Emerita of the History of Art at Northern Illinois University, is author of *Rome Is Love Spelled Backward: Enjoying Art and Architecture in the Eternal City*, 1998, as cited on "Roman Jews and the Arch of Titus," *Robert Kahn's Blog*, July 25, 2011)

Some other quotes:

"Now when Titus was come into this [upper] city, he admired not only some other

places of strength in it, but particularly those strong towers which the tyrants in their mad conduct had relinquished; for when he saw their solid altitude, and the largeness of their several stones, and the exactness of their joints, as also how great was their breadth, and how extensive their length, he expressed himself after the manner following: 'We have certainly had God for our assistant in this war, and it was no other than God who ejected the Jews out of these fortifications; for what could the hands of men or any machines do towards overthrowing these towers?'" (Josephus, *War of the Jews*, 6.9.1)

"After [Vespasian's son] Titus had taken Jerusalem, and when the country all round was filled with corpses, the neighboring races offered him a crown; but he disclaimed any such honor to himself, saying that it was not himself that had accomplished this exploit, but that he had merely lent his arms to God, who had so manifested his wrath; and Apollonius praised his action, for therein he displayed a great deal of judgment and understanding of things human and divine, and it showed great moderation on his part that he refused to be crowned because he had shed blood." (Philostratus, *The Life of Apollonius of Tyana*, 6.29)

This begs the question, if the "temple" spoken of by Paul in his **Man of Sin** prophecy of 2 Thessalonians 2 is our body and the body of believers and not a yet to be built physical temple by the Jews, then what was the **Abomination of Desolation** spoken of by Daniel and referenced by Jesus? A brief review of the **Abomination of Desolation** references will help.

Abomination of Desolation

These are all of the mentions of the *Abomination of Desolation*:

Abomination Desolate

31 And arms shall stand on his part, and they shall pollute the sanctuary of strength, and shall take away the daily sacrifice, and they **shall place the abomination that maketh desolate**. (Daniel 11)

11 And from the time that the daily sacrifice shall be taken away, and the **abomination that maketh desolate set up**, there shall be a thousand two hundred and ninety days. (Daniel 12)

Abomination Desolation

15 When ye therefore shall see the **abomination of desolation, spoken of by Daniel the prophet**, stand in the holy place. (Matthew 24)

15 "So when you see standing in the holy place '**the abomination that causes desolation**,' spoken of through the prophet Daniel - let the reader understand" (Matthew 24, NIV)

15 "Therefore when you see the '**abomination of desolation**,' spoken of by Daniel the prophet, standing in the holy place" (whoever reads, let him understand). (Matthew 24, NKJV)

15 So when you see the appalling sacrilege [the **abomination that astonishes and makes desolate**], spoken of by the prophet Daniel, standing in the Holy Place - let the reader take notice and ponder and consider and heed [this] (Matthew 24, AMP)

15 "Therefore when you see the **abomination of desolation** which was spoken of through Daniel the prophet, standing in the holy place (let the reader understand), (Matthew 24, NASB)

15-20 "But be ready to run for it when you see the **monster of desecration** set up in the Temple sanctuary. The prophet Daniel described this. If you've read Daniel, you'll know what I'm talking about. If you're living in Judea at the time, run for the hills; if you're working in the yard, don't return to the house to get anything; if you're out in the field, don't go back and get your coat. Pregnant and nursing mothers will have it especially hard. Hope and pray this won't happen during the winter or on a Sabbath. (Matthew 24, MSG)

14 But when ye shall see the **abomination of desolation, spoken of by Daniel the prophet**, standing where it ought not, (let him that readeth understand,) then let them that be in Judaea flee to the mountains. (Mark 13)

Abominations Desolate

29 Then shall they know that I am the LORD, when I have laid the land most **desolate** because of all their **abominations** which they have committed. (Ezekiel 33)

27 And he shall confirm the covenant with many for one week: and in the midst of the week he shall cause the sacrifice and the oblation to cease, and for the overspreading of **abominations he shall make it desolate, even until the consummation, AND that determined shall be poured upon the desolate**. (Daniel 9) *[The Abominations will continue after it has been consumed, i.e., from 70 A.D. until the antichrist shows up.]*

Abominations Desolation

22 So that the LORD could no longer bear, because of the evil of your doings, and because of the **abominations** which ye have committed; therefore is your land a **desolation**, and an astonishment, and a curse, without an inhabitant, as at this day. (Ezekiel 44)

We see that the words "abomination" and "desolation" have been used by other prophets in different combinations and that it is more of an expression then an identification.

Conclusion

To sum up, we learned that it was Roman paganism that overcame Judaism when Titus destroyed the temple in 70 A.D. - just as Jesus prophesied. The temple was looted of its implements which were taken back to Rome and the *Arch of Titus* still stands today as a commemoration of that event. Now that we know what the abomination was that laid waste to Jerusalem and Judaism, one question remains - what became of the abomination? Here I differ from other prophecy commentators in that I continue to follow the abomination knowing that behind it remained a spiritual ruler who was in no way through destroying the work of God.

A good question to ask is "Why weren't the Christians in Jerusalem destroyed?" Simple, the followers of Jesus had given heed to his warnings and left before the destruction came. No doubt the ruler of darkness was frustrated that he could not lay desolate the Christians at the same time he laid desolated the Jews. Not to worry, in a few short years he successfully laid waste to them in a different way by infiltrating them doctrinally with his abominations, thereby turning the "bride" of Christ into a "whore."

Whore

The symbol of a "woman" is used twice in *The Revelation of John*, one to represent evil, the other to represent good. The use of the female symbol to juxtapose the believers against the deceived is an interesting topic other commentators have not addressed. In truth, it is key for understanding the others prophecies.

Mentions

Rev. 12 - The Good

Here are the good references:

1 And there appeared a great wonder in heaven; a **woman** clothed with the sun, and the moon under her feet, and upon her head a crown of twelve stars:

4 And his tail drew the third part of the stars of heaven, and did cast them to the earth: and the dragon stood before the **woman** which was ready to be delivered, for to devour her child as soon as it was born.

6 And the **woman** fled into the wilderness, where she hath a place prepared of God, that they should feed her there a thousand two hundred and threescore days.

13 And when the dragon saw that he was cast unto the earth, he persecuted the **woman** which brought forth the man child.
14 And to the **woman** were given two wings of a great eagle, that she might fly into the wilderness, into her place, where she is nourished for a time, and times, and half a time, from the face of the serpent.
15 And the serpent cast out of his mouth water as a flood after the **woman**, that he might cause her to be carried away of the flood.
16 And the earth helped the **woman**, and the earth opened her mouth, and swallowed up the flood which the dragon cast out of his mouth.
17 And the dragon was wroth with the **woman**, and went to make war with the remnant of her seed, which keep the commandments of God, and have the testimony of Jesus Christ. (Revelation 12)

Rev. 17 - The Bad

Here are the bad references:

3 So he carried me away in the spirit into the wilderness: and I saw a **woman** sit upon a scarlet coloured beast, full of names of blasphemy, having seven heads and ten horns.
4 And the **woman** was arrayed in purple and scarlet colour, and decked with gold and precious stones and pearls, having a golden cup in her hand full of abominations and filthiness of her fornication:
5 And upon her forehead was a name written, MYSTERY, BABYLON THE GREAT, THE MOTHER OF HARLOTS AND

ABOMINATIONS OF THE EARTH.
6 And I saw the **woman** drunken with the blood of the saints, and with the blood of the martyrs of Jesus: and when I saw her, I wondered with great admiration.
7 And the angel said unto me, Wherefore didst thou marvel? I will tell thee the mystery of the **woman**, and of the beast that carrieth her, which hath the seven heads and ten horns.
8 The beast that thou sawest was, and is not; and shall ascend out of the bottomless pit, and go into perdition: and they that dwell on the earth shall wonder, whose names were not written in the book of life from the foundation of the world, when they behold the beast that was, and is not, and yet is.
9 And here is the mind which hath wisdom. The seven heads are seven mountains, on which the **woman** sitteth.
18 And the **woman** which thou sawest is that great city, which reigneth over the kings of the earth. (Revelation 17)

Symbolism

Woman = Caregiver

There are two churches depicted in John's Revelation: **The Woman** and **The Whore**. One represents the true followers of Jesus and the other the deceived.

Woman in Rev. 12

To better understand the "woman" verses of Revelation 12, a review of other women verses in the New Testament may help.

Jesus as Bridegroom

In the **Parable of the Ten Virgins** Jesus is represented as the **bridegroom**:

1 Then shall the kingdom of heaven be likened unto ten virgins, which took their lamps, and went forth to meet the **bridegroom**.
2 And five of them were wise, and five were foolish.
3 They that were foolish took their lamps, and took no oil with them:
4 But the wise took oil in their vessels with their lamps.
5 While the **bridegroom** tarried, they all slumbered and slept.
6 And at midnight there was a cry made, Behold, the **bridegroom** cometh; go ye out to meet him.
7 Then all those virgins arose, and trimmed their lamps.
8 And the foolish said unto the wise, Give us of your oil; for our lamps are gone out.
9 But the wise answered, saying, Not so; lest there be not enough for us and you: but go ye rather to them that sell, and buy for yourselves.
10 And while they went to buy, the **bridegroom** came; and they that were ready went in with him to the marriage: and the door was shut.
11 Afterward came also the other virgins, saying, Lord, Lord, open to us.
12 But he answered and said, Verily I say unto

you, I know you not.
13 **Watch therefore, for ye know neither the day nor the hour wherein the Son of man cometh.** (Matthew 25)

Jesus as Husband

Just as the man is the husband of the wife, so too is Christ the **husband** of the church:

23 For the **husband** is the **head of the wife**, even as **Christ** is the **head of the church**: and he is the **saviour of the body.** (Ephesians 5)

18 And **he is the head of the body, the church**. (Colossians 1)

Kingdom of Heaven

The first time that Jesus came, he preached all about the **Kingdom of God**:

14 Jesus came into Galilee, **preaching the gospel of the kingdom of God,**
15 And saying, The time is fulfilled, and the **kingdom of God is at hand**: repent ye, and believe the gospel. (Mark 1)

The disciples had great expectations for when the kingdom Jesus kept preaching about would come:

11 And as they heard these things, he added and spake a parable, because he was nigh to Jerusalem, and because **they thought that the kingdom of God should immediately appear.** (Luke 19)

6 When they therefore were come together, they asked of him, saying, Lord, **wilt thou at this time restore again the kingdom to Israel?**
7 And he said unto them, It is not for you to know the times or the seasons, which the Father hath put in his own power. (Acts 1)

Even though Jesus said the timing was not for them to know, he did recommend that they seek it and pray for it:

33 But **seek ye first the kingdom of God**, and his righteousness; and all these things shall be added unto you. (Matthew 6)

2 And he said unto them, When ye **pray**, say, Our Father which art in heaven, Hallowed be thy name. **Thy kingdom come.** (Luke 11)

The **Kingdom of God** will arrive just as soon as Satan is removed. First from heaven, i.e. the **Second Heaven**:

10 And I heard a loud voice saying in heaven, **Now is come** salvation, and strength, and **the kingdom of our God**, and the power of his Christ: **for the accuser of our brethren is cast down,** which accused them before our God day and night. (Revelation 12)

And then from earth:

15 And the seventh angel sounded; and there were great voices in heaven, saying, **The kingdoms of this world are become the kingdoms of our**

Lord, and of his Christ; and he shall reign for ever and ever. (Revelation 11)

The bride/church will return with Jesus and reign with him on earth:

10 And **hast made us unto our God kings and priests: and we shall reign on the earth.** (Revelation 5)

6 Blessed and holy is he that hath part in the first resurrection: on such the second death hath no power, but **they shall be priests of God and of Christ, and shall reign with him a thousand years.** (Revelation 20)

We will see that it is this expectation for the Kingdom of God and those who will **rule** it [Bride and Bridegroom] that are the birth pains described by John.

Rule

The **rule** theme is important for understanding who the **woman** and **man child** are. Both will rule through the millennium. Here are the rule references in John's Revelation:

26 And **he that overcometh**, and keepeth my works unto the end, to him **will I give power over the nations:**
27 And **he shall rule** them with a **rod of iron**; as the vessels of a potter shall they be broken to shivers: even as I received of my Father. (Revelation 2)

5 And she [the woman] brought forth a **man child**, who was to **rule all nations with a rod of iron:**

and her child was caught up unto God, and to his throne. (Revelation 12)

14 And the armies which were in heaven followed him upon white horses, clothed in fine linen, white and clean.
15 And out of his mouth goeth a sharp sword, that with it he should smite the nations: and **he shall rule them with a rod of iron.** (Revelation 19)

We see that there are two people who will **rule** through the **Millennium** - Jesus and the faithful. The woman represents the faithful believers, i.e. the five wise virgins in the **Parable of the Ten Virgins**. These God will remove until the antichrist finishes the task of chastising the unwise five virgins; the unfaithful and deceived.

Reign

The **reign** mentions confirm the **rule** mentions. This is why people use the dual expression **"rule and reign with Christ."**

1 Behold, a **king** [Jesus] shall **reign** in righteousness, and **princes** [faithful] shall **rule** in judgment. (Isaiah 32)

10 And **hast made us unto our God kings and priests: and we shall reign on the earth.** (Revelation 5)

6 Blessed and holy is he that hath part in the first resurrection: on such the second death hath no power, but **they shall be priests of God and of Christ, and shall reign with him a thousand years.** (Revelation 20)

Revelation 12

Here is the complete text:

1 And there appeared a great wonder in heaven; **a woman clothed with the sun**, and the **moon under her feet**, and upon her **head a crown of twelve stars:**
2 And she **being with child cried**, travailing in birth, and **pained to be delivered.**
3 And there appeared another wonder in heaven; and behold a great **red dragon,** having seven heads and ten horns, and seven crowns upon his heads.
4 And his tail drew the **third part of the stars of heaven**, and did **cast them to the earth:** and the **dragon stood before the woman** which was ready to be delivered, for to devour **her child** as soon as it was born.
5 And she brought forth **a man child, who was to rule all nations** with a **rod of iron;** and [after] her child was [born, he was] **caught up unto God, and to his throne.**
6 And the **woman fled into the wilderness,** where she hath a **place prepared of God**, that they should feed her there a **thousand two hundred and threescore days.**
7 And there was **war in heaven:** Michael and his angels fought against the dragon; and the dragon fought and his angels,
8 And prevailed not; **neither was their place found any more in heaven.**
9 And the **great dragon** was cast out, that **old serpent**, called the **Devil**, and **Satan**, which deceiveth the whole world: he was **cast out into**

the earth, and his angels were cast out with him.

10 And I heard a loud voice saying in heaven, **Now is come** salvation, and strength, and the **kingdom of our God**, and the power of his Christ: for the accuser of our brethren is cast down, which accused them before our God day and night.

11 And they overcame him by the blood of the Lamb, and by the word of their testimony; and they loved not their lives unto the death.

12 **Therefore rejoice, ye heavens, and ye that dwell in them.** Woe to the inhabiters of the earth and of the sea! for the **devil is come down unto you,** having great wrath, because he knoweth that he hath but a **short time.**

13 And when the **dragon** saw that he was *[would be]* cast unto the earth, he **persecuted the woman** which brought *[would bring]* forth the **man child.** *[YLT version.]*

14 And to the **woman were given two wings of a great eagle, that she might fly into the wilderness,** into **her place,** where she is **nourished** for a **time, and times, and half a time,** from the face of the serpent.

15 And the **serpent** cast out of his mouth **water as a flood** after the **woman**, that he might cause her to be **carried away of the flood.**

16 And the earth helped the **woman**, and the earth opened her mouth, and swallowed up the flood which the **dragon** cast out of his mouth.

17 And the **dragon** was wroth with the **woman**, and **went to make war with the remnant of her seed, which keep the commandments of God, and have the testimony of Jesus Christ.**

(Revelation 12)

Definitions

Woman = The Church or Believers.

Clothed with Sun = Sun is God's Glory or the Holy Spirit. The woman analogy applies to Spirit filled believers.

Moon = The ruler of darkness; Spirit filled believers have power over the evil one (Mark 16:16; Rev. 2:26).

Crown of 12 Stars = Twelve apostles. Literally, they are "the crown" of Believers.

Red Dragon = Satan

1/3 Stars = Stars represent angels. The one third represent Satan's angels.

Cast to earth = It has been great for Satan's angels to rule in high places (Daniel 10:13; Ephesians 6:12), but the time will come when they will lose those lofty stations and be forced to earth when Satan is cast out (Rev. 12:9).

Stood before the Woman = Put his attention against Christians, Spirit filled believers in particular (2 Timothy 3:12).

Man Child = The name "man child" juxtaposes who Jesus was with angels and Satan, who were never born, nor ever as a child.

Rod of Iron = Stern government. (Easton's *Bible Dictionary*)

Caught Up = Jesus was God; at no time did he need to be "rescued." A better wording is *Young's Literal Translation*:

> **And she brought forth a male child, who is about to rule all the nations with a rod of iron, and caught away was her child unto God and His throne.** (Rev. 12:5, YLT)

Woman fled = Raptured. See v. 14 "given two wings of an eagle."

Place prepared = A temporary place until the faithful return to reign with Jesus. Where is it: *"He that overcometh. ...I will give him the morning star. (Venus; heavenly side.)"* (Rev. 2:28)

1260 Days = Also expressed as *48 months*; or, *a times, time, and half time (v. 14)*; which is the same amount of time allotted to:

a. Satan [Once cast down.]

b. Two Witnesses

War in heaven = This war has not happened. **Jesus** saw **Satan** fall from the **Third Heaven. Satan** still remains in the **Second Heaven**. The **First Heaven** is our sky, that dimension we see. The next dimension is the **Second Heaven**, and where God resides is the highest or **Third Heaven. Satan** will yet be removed from the **Second Heaven** and cast unto the earth.

Their place = This phrase is usually read "there" place, but it is actually "their": **neither was there/their place found any more in heaven.** What does "their place" look like?

Kingdom of God = Once Satan and his angels are removed from heaven (that is the Second Heaven), the Kingdom of God will take its place. Then "the inhabitants" there "will rejoice." The Kingdom of God will not come down to earth until Satan is removed. Those on earth likewise will not be able to "rejoice" until he is removed from there.

Flood = Water is a diluter. The evil one knows the scriptures; he knows he will be cast to earth. He knows the Woman, who is The Church, will produce rulers, who will reign with Jesus. To limit that number, he has sought to dilute the gospel with false teachings. The "earth" has absorbed many of them over time by way of the elements: fires, floods, rains, wars, etc.

Remnant = Who are the "remnant" Satan will "make war with"? These are the other **Five Virgins**, the unfaithful ones. These are deceived, slack, or lazy Christians whom Jesus identified in the **Seven Churches**, who will suffer God's wrath in the **End Time Challenges**.

In Parallel

Many scriptural topics receive emphasis through the use of a literary device called **Chiasmus**.[9] The following example demonstrates a **chiasmus in parallel**. This topic is of the woman fleeing into the wilderness. If wrongly read as two separate events John's Revelation could be greatly skewed.

Revelation 12:6 **Revelation 12:14**

6 And the woman fled into the wilderness where she hath a place prepared of God that they should feed her there a thousand two hundred and threescore days.	14 And to the woman were given two wings of a great eagle that she might fly into the wilderness into her place where she is nourished for a time and times and half a time from the face of the serpent.
The Breakdown	**The Breakdown**
6 the woman	14 the woman
6 fled	14 were given two wings of a great eagle that she might fly
6 into the wilderness	14 into the wilderness
6 where she hath a place prepared of God	14 into her place

6 that they should feed her there	14 where she is nourished
6 a thousand two hundred and threescore days	14 for a time, and times, and half a time

Whore in Rev. 17

The "whore" is the antithesis of the "woman." The symbolism of the whore is detailed next:

1 And there came one of the seven angels which had the seven vials, and talked with me, saying unto me, Come hither; I will shew unto thee the judgment of the **great whore** that **sitteth upon many waters:**
2 With whom the **kings of the earth have committed fornication**, and the **inhabitants of the earth have been made drunk with the wine of her fornication.**
3 So he carried me away in the spirit into the wilderness: and I saw a **woman sit** upon a **scarlet coloured beast,** full of **names of blasphemy**, having **seven heads** and **ten horns**.
4 And the **woman was arrayed in purple and scarlet colour, and decked with gold and precious stones and pearls, having a golden cup in her hand full of abominations and filthiness of her fornication:**

5 **And upon her forehead was a name written, MYSTERY, BABYLON THE GREAT, THE MOTHER OF HARLOTS AND ABOMINATIONS OF THE EARTH.**
6 And I saw the **woman drunken with the blood of the saints, and with the blood of the martyrs of Jesus:** and when I saw her, I wondered with great admiration.
7 And the angel said unto me, Wherefore didst thou marvel? I will tell thee the mystery of the **woman**, and of the **beast that carrieth her**, which hath the **seven heads** and **ten horns.**
8 The **beast** that thou sawest **was, and is not; and shall ascend out of the bottomless pit, and go into perdition: and they that dwell on the earth shall wonder, whose names were not written in the book of life** from the foundation of the world, when they behold the **beast** that was, and is not, and yet is.
9 And here is the mind which hath wisdom. The **seven heads are seven mountains, on which the woman sitteth.**
10 And **there are seven kings: five are fallen, and one is, and the other is not yet come; and when he cometh, he must continue a short space.**
11 And the **beast that was, and is not, even he is the eighth**, and is of the seven, and goeth into perdition.
12 And the **ten horns which thou sawest are ten kings, which have received no kingdom as yet; but receive power as kings one hour with the beast.**
13 These have one mind, and **shall give their**

power and strength unto the beast.
14 These **shall make war with the Lamb**, and the Lamb shall overcome them: for he is Lord of lords, and King of kings: and they that are with him are called, and chosen, and faithful.
15 And he saith unto me, **The waters which thou sawest, where the whore sitteth, are peoples, and multitudes, and nations, and tongues.**
16 And the **ten horns which thou sawest upon the beast, these shall hate the whore, and shall make her desolate and naked, and shall eat her flesh, and burn her with fire.**
17 For God hath put in their hearts to fulfil his will, and to agree, and give their kingdom unto the **beast**, until the words of God shall be fulfilled.
18 And the **woman which thou sawest is that great city, which reigneth over the kings of the earth.** (Revelation 17)

Great City

18 And the **woman which thou sawest is that great city, which reigneth over the kings of the earth.** (Revelation 17)

Vatican - St Peter Square

Purple, Scarlet, Gold, Stones

4 And the woman was arrayed in **purple** and **scarlet colour**, and decked with **gold** and **precious stones** (Revelation 17)

The pictures on the right speak for themselves.

"The Triregnum, the Papal Tiara formed by three crowns symbolizing the triple power of the Pope: father of kings, governor of the world and Vicar (substitute) of Christ."[10]

There is but one "father of kings":

> And he hath on his vesture and on his thigh a name written, **KING OF KINGS**, AND LORD OF LORDS. (Revelation 19)

This description is nearly word-for-word of when Emperor Constantine asserted leadership over the Church:

> As soon, then, as the whole assembly had seated themselves with becoming gravity, a general silence prevailed, in expectation of the emperor's arrival. And first of all three of his immediate family entered in succession, and others also preceded his approach, not of the soldiers or guards who usually accompanied him, but only friends who avowed the faith of Christ. And now, all rising at the signal which indicated the emperor's entrance, at last **he himself proceeded through the midst of the assembly, like some heavenly messenger of God, clothed in raiment which glittered as it were with rays of light, reflecting the glowing radiance of a PURPLE ROBE, and adorned with the brilliant splendor of GOLD and PRECIOUS STONES.** Such was the external appearance of his person; and with regard to his mind, it was evident that he was distinguished by piety and godly fear. This was indicated by his downcast eyes, the blush on his countenance, and the modesty of his gait. For the rest of his personal excellencies, he surpassed all present in height of stature and beauty of form, as well as in majestic dignity of men, and invincible strength and vigor. All

these graces, united to a suavity of manner, and a serenity becoming his imperial station, declared the excellence of his mental qualities to be above all praise. As soon as he had advanced to the upper end of the seats, at first he remained standing, and when a low chair of wrought gold had been set for him, he waited until the bishops had beckoned to him, and then sat down, and after him the whole assembly did the same. (EUSEBIUS PAMPHILUS, *ECCLESIASTICAL HISTORY. THE LIFE OF THE BLESSED EMPEROR CONSTANTINE, IN FOUR BOOKS, FROM 306 TO 337 A.D.*, LONDON: SAMUEL BAGSTER AND SONS, 1845 pp. 122-123.)

Golden Cup

4. ..having a **golden cup** in her hand full of abominations and filthiness of her fornication: (Revelation 17)

Indeed, if the Eucharist, as performed by the Roman Catholic Church using golden goblets/chalices inlaid with jewels are believed to contain the actual blood of Jesus through a process called **transubstantiation** whereby our Lord is re-crucified, then that may be the cup John the Revelator saw.

> In 1551, the Council of Trent officially defined that 'by the consecration of the bread and wine there takes place a change of the whole substance of the bread into the substance of the body of Christ our Lord and of the whole substance of the wine into the substance of his blood. This change the holy Catholic Church has fittingly and properly called **transubstantiation**.' (Council of Trent, Session

XIII, chapter IV; cf. canon II)

In line with this definition, rejection of the doctrine of transubstantiation was considered heresy during the five-year reign (1553-1558) of Mary I of England. John Frith, John Rogers, and Rowland Taylor were executed for refusing to accept it, as recounted in *Foxe's Book of Martyrs.* Mary's successor Elizabeth declared that: 'Transubstantiation (or the change of the substance of Bread and Wine) in the Supper of the Lord, cannot be proved by holy Writ; but is repugnant to the plain words of Scripture, overthroweth the nature of a Sacrament, and hath given occasion to many superstitions and made assistance at Mass illegal.'[11]

Abomination

Greek: bdelugma, bdel'-oog-mah
Definition: a detestation, i.e. (spec.) idolatry
Translated: abomination. (James Strong, *Lexicon of the Greek New Testament*)

This word is also used symbolically of sin in general (Isa. 66:3); an idol (44:19); the ceremonies of the apostate Church of Rome (Rev. 17:4); a detestable act (Ezek. 22:11). (M. G. Easton, *Illustrated Bible Dictionary*)

Fornication

Greek: porneia, por-ni'-ah
Definition: harlotry (include adultery and incest); fig. idolatry

Translated: fornication. (James Strong, *Lexicon of the Greek New Testament*)

In every form of it was sternly condemned by the Mosaic law (Lev. 21:9; 19:29; Deut. 22:20, 21, 23-29; 23:18; Ex. 22:16). But this word is more frequently used in a symbolical way than in its ordinary sense. It frequently means a forsaking of God or a following after idols (Isa. 1:2; Jer. 2:20; Ezek. 16; Hos. 1:2; 2:1-5; Jer. 3:8, 9). (M. G. Easton, *Illustrated Bible Dictionary*)

Nations

1 great whore that sitteth upon many waters:
2 the inhabitants of the earth have been made drunk with the wine of her fornication.
15 And he saith unto me, The waters which thou sawest, where the whore sitteth, are peoples, and multitudes, and **nations**, and tongues (Revelation 17)

Her influence extends to all nations, peoples, tongues, and multitudes:

1.196 billion or 17% of the world population

93,000 elementary schools

44,000 secondary schools

413,000 priests

722,000 religious sisters

75 million students in Catholic schools.[12]

The Holy See of the Roman Church has Diplomatic Relations with 179 Nations.[13]

The Holy See Participates in many International Organizations.[14]

Kings

2 With whom the **kings of the earth** have committed fornication

18 And the woman which thou sawest is that great city, which reigneth over the **kings of the earth**. (Revelation 17)

The Roman Church can wield influence over the rulers of the earth via her members. She can use them to influence the outcome of elections.

Hitler at New Year's Reception in the Chancellery & Vatican Minister. Photo by Hugo Jaeger.

Her relationship with these kings is called

fornication or translated thus:

Immorality (NASB)

Whoredom (YLT)

Idolatry (AMP)

Abominations

> 5 And upon her forehead was a name written, MYSTERY, BABYLON THE GREAT, THE MOTHER OF HARLOTS AND ABOMINATIONS OF THE EARTH. (Revelation 17)

Her titles include: **Mystery**, **Babylon the Great,** and **Mother of Harlots & Abominations**.

Titles of the Pope

> 1. The Pope is of so great dignity and so exalted that **he is not mere man, but as it were God**, and the vicar of God.
> 12. He is likewise the divine monarch, and **supreme emperor**, and **king of kings**.
> 13. Hence the Pope is crowned with a triple crown, as **king of heaven** and of earth and of hell.
> 14. Moreover the superiority and the power of the Roman Pontiff by no means pertains only to heavenly things, but **also earthly things**, and to things under the earth, and even over the angels, whom he is greater than.
> 18. As to papal authority, the **Pope is as it were God on earth**, Sole sovereign of all the faithful of

Christ, **chief king of kings**, having a plentitude of unbroken power, entrusted by the omnipotent God to govern the earthly and heavenly kingdoms.
30. The Pope is of so great authority and power, that **he is able to modify, declare, or interpret even divine laws**.[15]

Luther

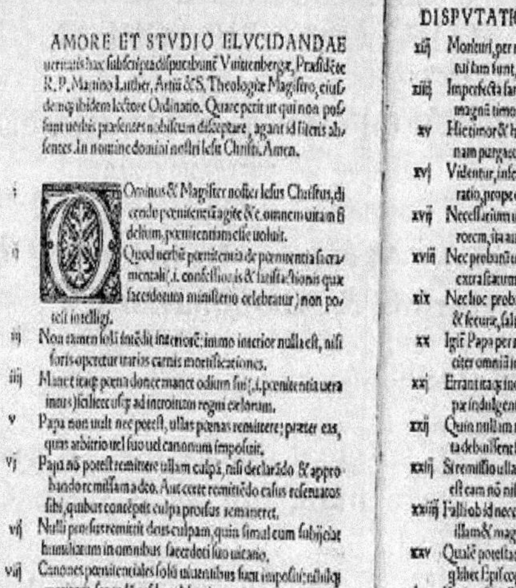
AMORE ET STVDIO ELVCIDANDAE

DISPVTATIO DE VIRTVTE INDVLGEN.

Martin Luther 95 Theses

Martin Luther wrote a Theses listing 95 points

against the Roman Catholic Church. To wit - that the Pope claimed to be able to pardon sins and remove the repentance process by money.

The Pope likewise claimed to be able to free souls from "Purgatory" - with money:

Examples:

5. The pope does not intend to remit, and cannot remit any penalties other than those which he has imposed either by his own authority or by that of the Canons.

21. Therefore those preachers of indulgences are in error, who say that by the **pope's indulgences a man is freed from every penalty, and saved;**

27. They preach man who say that so **soon as the penny jingles into the money-box, the soul flies out [of purgatory].**

32. They will be condemned eternally, together with their teachers, who **believe themselves sure of their salvation because they have letters of pardon.**

36. Every truly repentant Christian has a right to full remission of penalty and guilt, even without letters of pardon.

40. **True contrition seeks and loves penalties**, but liberal pardons only relax penalties and cause them to be hated, or at least, furnish an occasion [for hating them].

82. **Why does not the pope empty purgatory,** for the sake of holy love and of the dire need of the souls that are there, if he redeems an infinite

number of souls for the sake of **miserable money with which to build a Church?**

86. Why does not the pope, **whose wealth is today greater than the riches of the richest**, build just this one church of St. Peter with his own money, **rather than with the money of poor believers?**

Her abominations include putting priest and pope before God and Christ. The free gift that Jesus brought is held captive by an old Old Testament framework that uses a third party intercessor other than Jesus. That, in reality, is antichrist, for it works contrary to Christ.

Martyrs

6 And **I saw the woman drunken with the blood of the saints, and with the blood of the martyrs of Jesus**: and when I saw her, I wondered with great admiration. (Revelation 17)

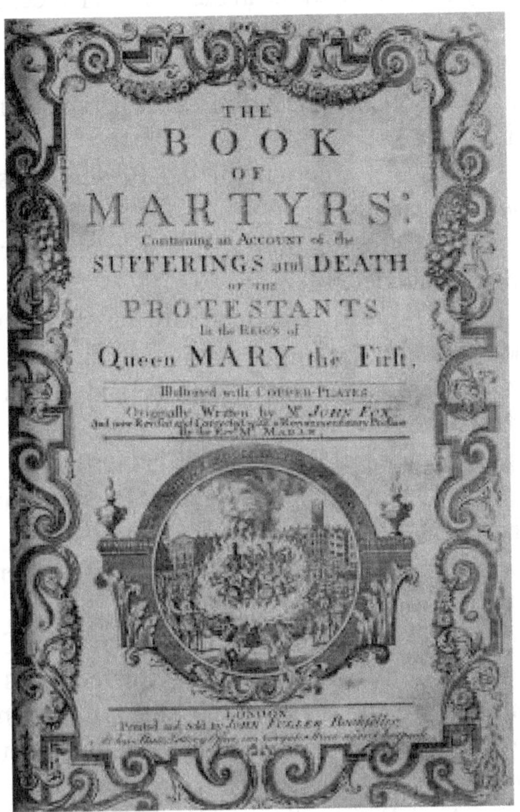
THE
BOOK
OF
MARTYRS:
Containing an ACCOUNT of the
SUFFERINGS and DEATH
OF THE
PROTESTANTS
In the REIGN of
Queen MARY the First,
Illustrated with COPPER-PLATES.
Originally Written by Mr JOHN FOX
LONDON

Foxe

Foxe's *Book of Martyrs* lays out many of the atrocities committed by the Roman Catholic Church. She is full of the blood of the saints and the Roman Empire before her is full of the blood of the apostles.

Preface
Chapter I History of Christian Martyrs to the First General Persecutions Under Nero
Chapter II The Ten Primitive Persecutions

the South of France, During the Years 1814 and 1820
Chapter XXII The Beginnings of American Foreign Missions
Epilogue to the original edition

Beast

The whore is "carried" on a "beast" who has **seven heads** and **ten horns**.

Symbolic

3 So he carried me away in the spirit into the wilderness: and I saw a woman sit upon a scarlet coloured beast, full of names of blasphemy, having **seven heads** and **ten horns**.

9 And here is the mind which hath wisdom. The **seven heads** are **seven mountains,** on which the woman sitteth.

12 And the **ten horns** which thou sawest are **ten kings**, which have received no kingdom as yet; but receive power as kings one hour with the beast.

(Revelation 17)

Seven Heads

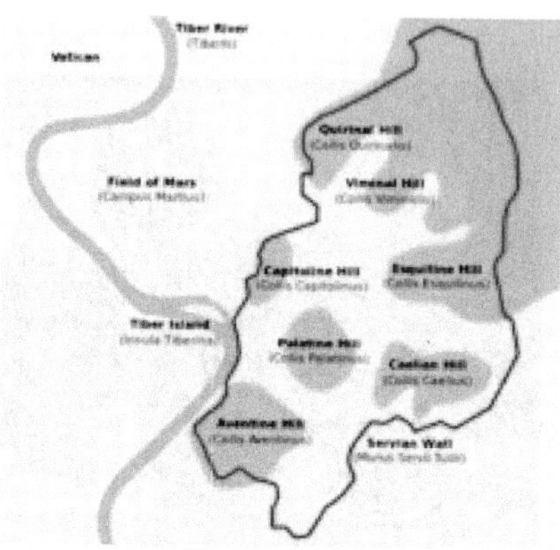

Seven Hills of Rome

The above verses give the meaning of the symbols:

Seven Heads = Hills or mountains where the whore resides.

The City of Rome was built within in seven hills which provided a great deal of protection.

Ten Horns

Ten Horns = Ten kings who are not yet, but will become such after the beast corporal arrives.

Corporal

The "beast" corporal is mentioned here:

10 And there are seven kings: five are fallen, and
one is, and **the other is not yet come;** and when

he cometh, he must continue a **short space.**
11 And the **beast** that was, and is not, even **he is the eighth**, and is of the seven, and goeth into perdition. (Revelation 17)

We learn there is an actual beast corporal and it will be the eighth and last king. This scenario was prophesied of by the prophet Daniel.

Daniel

The "fourth beast" of Daniel is the same as the "beast with seven heads and ten horns" of John and the "corporal" beast of John, i.e. the "eighth king" is the same as the "little horn" of Daniel:

The Roman Church can (and has) wield influence over the rulers of the earth directly or indirectly via its members. She uses them to affect the outcome of elections and therefore has control over kings and rulers indirectly. Her relationship with these kings is called **fornication.** Other translations for **fornication** are:

Immorality (NASB)

Whoredom (YLT)

Idolatry (AMP)

Abomination

7 After this I saw in the night visions and behold a **fourth beast**, dreadful and terrible, and strong exceedingly; and it had great iron teeth: it devoured and brake in pieces, and stamped the residue with the feet of it: and it was diverse from all the beasts

that were before it; and **it had ten horns.**
8 I considered the horns, and, behold, **there came up among them** another **little horn**, before whom there were three of the first horns plucked up by the roots: and, behold, in this horn were eyes like the eyes of man, and a mouth speaking great things.

23 Thus he said, The fourth beast shall be the fourth kingdom upon earth, which shall be diverse from all kingdoms, and shall devour the whole earth, and shall tread it down, and break it in pieces.
24 And the **ten horns** out of this kingdom are **ten kings** that shall arise: and **another shall rise after them**; and he shall be diverse from the first, and he shall subdue three kings.
25 And he shall speak great words against the most High, and shall wear out the saints of the most High, and think to change times and laws: and they shall be given into his hand until a time and times and the dividing of time. (Daniel 7)

The ten kings will support a final ruler described by John as "beast" (corporal) and by Daniel as the "little horn" who rises "among them" and "after" them because he needs their support in order to emerge into the public.

Antichrist

They are both describing the prophesied antichrist.

Blasphemy

The "speak great words against the most High" by Daniel (7:25) is the same as "shall make war with the

Lamb" (Rev. 17:14) and "shall hate the whore [Catholicism]" (Rev. 17:16) of John. They are describing the antichrist.

Time

The "time and times and the dividing of time" of Daniel (7:25) is the same as:

> 12 Woe to the inhabiters of the earth and of the sea! for the devil is come down unto you, having great wrath, because he knoweth that he hath but a short time. (Revelation 12)
>
> 3 And I will give power unto my **Two Witnesses**, and they shall **prophesy a thousand two hundred and threescore days**, clothed in sackcloth. (Revelation 11)
>
> 14 And to the woman were given two wings of a great eagle, that she might fly into the wilderness, into her place, where she is nourished for a time, and times, and half a time, from the face of the serpent. (Revelation 12)
>
> 4 And they worshipped the dragon which gave power unto the beast: and they worshipped the beast, saying, Who is like unto the beast? who is able to make war with him?
> 5 And there was given unto him a mouth speaking great things and blasphemies; and power was given unto him to continue forty and two months.
> 6 And he opened his mouth in blasphemy against God, to blaspheme his name, and his tabernacle, and them that dwell in heaven.
> 7 And it was given unto him to make war with the saints, and to overcome them: and power was

given him over all kindreds, and tongues, and nations. (Revelation 13)

***Time* = 1 year (12 months / 360 days)**

***Times* = 2 year (24 months / 720 days)**

***Dividing time* = 6 months (180 days)**

***Time + times + dividing of time* = 1260 days**

***Thousand two hundred three score days* = 1260 days**

***42 months* = 1260 days**

Was

The "beast" is described as the beast "that **was**, and is not, and yet is." The woman is simply being *used* or *carried* for a time. The woman will be destroyed by the very "beast" (and its future ten kings) she has been riding. The beast is/was the *Roman Empire*.

The beast was smart to get on the "Christian band wagon" while it could - through Constantine. By doing so, the beast remained in control. That is why it says the beast "carried" the woman, the beast was in control and calling the shots. Her fruits were the same [continued to kill true believers] but now she was in control of the church, she could pollute it and use it to acquire wealth, influence, and control of the world - like she had before as the *Roman Empire*.

Pagan Christianity

Pagan Christianity is the title of a book produced by Frank Viola and George Barna. (Frank Viola and George Barna, *Pagan Christianity: Exploring the Roots of Our Church Practices*, Barna Books, 2008.) In it, they trace the origins of many of our Christian practices - *this* is the abomination that infiltrated the body of Christ.

Pagan Christianity leads readers on a fascinating tour through church history, revealing this startling and unsettling truth: Many cherished church traditions embraced today originated not out of the New Testament, but out of pagan (Greco-Roman) practices. This fact removes these cherished practices from the sacred and untouchable. But more than that, the book demonstrates that many of these cherished church traditions violate the teachings of Jesus and the apostles. (http://www.paganchristianity.org)

Sampling

1. The Church Building - first constructed around AD 327 and were patterned after the Roman basilicas which were patterned after the Greek temples.
2. Tax Exempt - Like pagan priests, Constantine gave the clergy tax-exemption in AD 313 and Christian churches tax-exemption in AD 323.
3. Hierarchical Leadership - Constantine, 4th

century, followed the pattern of the Babylonians, Persians, Greeks, and Romans.
4. Pastor
5. Clergy Attire - AD 330, Christian clergy started wearing the garb of Roman officials.
6. Choir - 4th century by Constantine to mimic the Roman Imperial ceremonies.
7. Tithing - Origin taken from the 10 percent rent charge used in the Roman Empire, justified by the Old Testament.
8. Clergy Salaries - Constantine, 4th century.
9. Infant Baptism - Rooted in the superstitious beliefs that pervaded the Greco-Roman culture, it was brought into the Christian faith in the late second century. By the fifth century, it replaced adult baptism.
10. Seminary - Council of Trent (1545-1563); Protestant, Massachusetts 1808; Bible College, D. L. Moody, 1882; Sunday School, Robert Raikes, Britain, 1780.
11. Youth Pastor - 1930, to meet needs of a new sociological class called teenagers.
12. Paul's Letters - combined and arranged according to size, 2nd century.

Extracts

-To be a Christian under Constantine's reign was no longer a handicap. It was an advantage. (p. 120)
-Clergymen received the same honors as the highest officials of the Roman Empire and even the

emperor himself. In fact, Constantine gave the bishops of Rome more power than he gave Roman governors. He also ordered that the **clergy receive fixed annual allowances (ministerial pay).** (p. 120)

-In AD 313, he **exempted the Christian clergy from paying taxes** - something that pagan priests had traditionally enjoyed. (fn. Hanson, *Christian Priesthood Examined,* p. 62; Durant, *Caesar and Christ,* pp. 656-657, 668.) He also made them exempt from mandatory public office and other civic duties. (fn. Duchesne, *Early History of the Christian Church,* p. 50; Johnson, *History of Christianity,* p. 77; Fox, *Pagans and Christians,* p. 667.) (p. 120)

-In all these things the clergy was given **special class status.** (p. 121)

-The clergy had the prestige of church office bearers, the privileges of a favored class, and the power of a wealthy elite. (p. 121)

-They even **dressed and groomed differently** from the common people. (fn. The bishop's dress was the ancient robe of a Roman magistrate. Clergy were not to let their hair grow long like the pagan philosophers (Hatch, *Organization of the Early Christian Churches,* pp. 164-165) Bishops and priests shaved their heads. This practice, known as the tonsure, comes from the old Roman ceremony of adoption. (p. 121)

-To their minds, being a church officer had become **more of a career than a calling.** (fn. Niebuhr and Williams, *Ministry in Historical Perspectives,* p. 29.) (p. 121)

-Clergymen were the trained leaders of the church

- the guardians of orthodoxy - the rulers and teachers of the people. They possessed gifts and graces not available to lesser mortals. **The laity were the second-class**, untrained Christians. The great theologian Karl Barth rightly said, **"The term 'laity' is one of the worst in the vocabulary of religion and ought to be banished from the Christian conversation.** (fn. Karl Barth, *Theologische Fragen und Antworten* (1957), pp. 183-184, quoted in R. J. Erler and R. Marquard, eds., *A Karl Barth Reader,* trans. G. W. Bromiley (Grand Rapids: Eerdmans, 1986), pp. 8-9.) (p. 122)

-This false dichotomy led to the profoundly mistaken idea that there are sacred professions (a call to "the ministry") and ordinary professions (a call to a worldly vocation). Historian Philip Schaff rightly describes these factors as creating **"the secularization of the church" where the "pure stream of Christianity" had become polluted.** Take note that this mistaken dichotomy still lives in the minds of many believers today. But the concept is pagan, not Christian. **It ruptures the New Testament reality that everyday life is sanctified by God.** (fn. Dunn, *New Testament Theology in Dialogue*, p. 127.) (pp. 122-123)

-During the third century, *ordination* took on an entirely different meaning. It was a formalized Christian rite. By the fourth century, the ceremony of ordination was embellished by symbolic garments and solemn ritual. **Ordination produced an ecclesiastical caste that usurped the believing priesthood.** (p. 124)

-From where did Christians get their pattern of ordination? They patterned their ordination ceremony after the Roman custom of appointing men to civil office. The entire process, down to the very words, came straight from the Roman civic world. (fn. Hatch, *Organization of the Early Christian Churches,* pp. 129-133. This same tendency was picked up by Judaism as early as the first century. Jewish scribes who were proficient in the interpretation of the Torah and the oral traditions ordained men for office in the Sanhedrin. These men were viewed as mediators of the will of God to all of Israel. The "ordained" of the Sanhedrin became so powerful that by the early second century the Romans put to death anyone who performed Jewish ordination! Warkentin, *Ordination: A Biblical-Historical View,* p. 16, 21-23, 25.) (p. 125)

-The forms of the Old Testament priesthood were combined with Greek hierarchy. (fn. Warkentin, *Ordination: A Biblical-Historical View,* p. 35. This is evident from the *Apostolic Constitutions,* AD 350-375) (p. 125)

-Christian ordination, then, came to be understood as that which constitutes the essential difference between clergy and laity. (p. 125)

-Eduard Schweizer, in his classic work *Church Order in the New Testament*, argues that **Paul knew nothing about an ordination that confers ministerial or clerical powers to a Christian.** (fn. Schweizer, *Church Order in the New Testament,* p. 207.) **First-century shepherds**

(elders, overseers) did not receive anything that resembles modern-day ordination. They were not set above the rest of the flock. They were those who served among them (see Acts 20:28, NASB, and 1 Peter 5:2-3, NASB). (p. 126)

-The contemporary practice of ordination creates a special caste of Christian. Whether it be the priest in Catholicism or the pastor in Protestantism, the result is the same: **The most important ministry is restricted to a few "special" believers. Such an idea is as damaging as it is no scriptural. The New Testament nowhere limits preaching, baptizing, or distributing the Lord's Supper to the "ordained."** Eminent scholar James D. G. Dunn put it best when he said that **the clergy-laity tradition has done more to undermine New Testament authority than most heresies.** (fn. Hanson, *Christian Priesthood Examined,* p. 82.) (p. 127)

-fn. 135 The **net effect is that modern ordination sets up artificial barriers between Christians and hinders mutual ministry. (p. 127)**

-Like the Catholic priest, the Reformed minister was viewed by the church as the "man of God" - the **paid mediator between God and His people.** He was not a mediator to forgive sins, but a mediator to communicate the divine will. **So in Protestantism an old problem took on a new form.** The jargon changed, but the error remained. (p. 129)

-Both the Reformers and the Puritans held the idea

that God's ministers must be competent professionals. Therefore, pastors had to undergo extensive academic training to fulfill their office. (fn. Hall, *Faithful Shepherd,* pp. 28-29.) (p. 130)

Notes

A reader can extract from the New Testament what Jesus taught and practiced. Jesus did not instruct anyone to build a physical church, nor did he command his apostles to build one. The practice is nowhere endorsed in the New Testament. Paul, who planted more churches, wrote most of the New Testament and lived longer than any other apostle (ministering over 30 years) never built a single church.

The *Institutionalization* of the gospel with pagan practices began with Constantine and the fruit was prophesied of:

> 1 And there came one of the seven angels which had the seven vials, and talked with me, saying unto me, Come hither; I will shew unto thee the judgment of the great whore that sitteth upon many waters:
> 2 **With whom the kings of the earth have committed fornication**, and the inhabitants of the earth have been made drunk with the wine of her fornication.
> 3 So he carried me away in the spirit into the wilderness: and **I saw a woman** sit upon a **scarlet coloured beast**, full of names of blasphemy, having seven heads and ten horns.

> 4 And **the woman was arrayed in PURPLE** and **scarlet** colour, and decked with **GOLD** and **PRECIOUS STONES** and **pearls**, having a **golden cup in her hand FULL OF ABOMINATIONS** and **filthiness** of her **fornication**:
> 5 And upon her forehead was a name written, MYSTERY, BABYLON THE GREAT, THE MOTHER OF HARLOTS AND **ABOMINATIONS** OF THE EARTH.
> 6 And I saw the woman **drunken with the blood of the saints**, and with the **blood of the martyrs of Jesus**: and when I saw her, I wondered with great admiration. (Revelation 17)

This description is nearly word-for-word of when Emperor Constantine asserted leadership over the body of Christ and the resulting fruit of Romanism (before him and after him), which was responsible for both the blood of the Saints and Martyrs of Jesus.

Constantine

At a gathering of some 250 bishops, historian Eusebius gave the following account:

> He gave from his own private resources costly benefactions to the Churches of God, both enlarging and heightening the sacred edifices, and **embellishing the august sanctuaries of the Church with abundant offerings.** (Eusebius Pamphilus, *Ecclesiastical History, The Life of the Blessed Emperor Constantine, in Four Books,*

From 306 to 337 A.D., London: Samuel Bagster and Sons, 1845, p. 37.)

As soon, then, as the whole assembly had seated themselves with becoming gravity, a general silence prevailed, in expectation of the emperor's arrival. And first of all three of his immediate family entered in succession, and others also preceded his approach, not of the soldiers or guards who usually accompanied him, but only friends who avowed the faith of Christ. And now, all rising at the signal which indicated the emperor's entrance, at last he himself proceeded through the midst of the assembly, **like some heavenly messenger of God, clothed in raiment which glittered as it were with rays of light, reflecting the glowing radiance of a PURPLE ROBE, and adorned with the brilliant splendor of GOLD and PRECIOUS STONES.** Such was the external appearance of his person; and with regard to his mind, it was evident that he was distinguished by piety and godly fear. This was indicated by his downcast eyes, the blush on his countenance, and the modesty of his gait. For the rest of his personal excellencies, he surpassed all present in height of stature and beauty of form, as well as in majestic dignity of men, and invincible strength and vigor. All these graces, united to a suavity of manner, and a serenity becoming his imperial station, declared the excellence of his mental qualities to be above all praise. As soon as he had advanced to the upper end of the seats, at first he remained standing, and when a low **chair of wrought gold had been set for him**, he waited until the bishops had beckoned to him, and then sat down, and after him the whole assembly did the same. (pp. 122-123.)

Churches have adorned their edifices ever since.

The "beast" is described as the beast "that **was**, and is not, and yet is." The woman is simply being *used* or *carried* for a time. The woman will be destroyed by the very "beast" (and its future ten kings) she has been riding. The beast is/was the *Roman Empire*.

The beast was smart to get on the "Christian band wagon" while it could - through Constantine. By doing so, the beast remained in control. That is why it says the beast "carried" the woman, the beast was in control and calling the shots. Her fruits were the same [continued to kill true believers] but now she was in control of the church, she could pollute it and use it to acquire wealth, influence, and control of the world - like she had before as the *Roman Empire*.

Babylon

Babylon, with its different physical and spiritual stages was shown to King Nebuchadnezzar in a dream and subsequently interpreted by Daniel the prophet. It would extend to the end of days in one form or another, guided by beings from the *Second Heaven.*

Hebrew

Bâbel, baw-bel'
Definition: *confusion*; *Babel* (i.e. Babylon), including Babylonia and the Bab. empire.
Translated as: Babel, Babylon. (James Strong, *Lexicon of the Hebrew Bible)*

Easton's Bible Dictionary

Babylon The Greek form of BABEL; Semitic form Babilu, meaning "The Gate of God." In the Assyrian tablets it means "The city of the dispersion of the tribes." The monumental list of its kings **reaches back to B.C. 2300**, and includes Khammurabi, or Amraphel (q.v.), the contemporary of Abraham. It stood on the Euphrates, about 200 miles above its junction with the Tigris, which flowed through its midst and divided it into two almost equal parts. The Elamites invaded Chaldea (i.e., Lower Mesopotamia, or Shinar, and Upper Mesopotamia, or Accad, now combined into one) and held it in subjection. At length Khammu-rabi delivered it from the foreign yoke, and founded the new empire of Chaldea (q.v.), making Babylon the capital of the united kingdom. This city gradually grew in extent and grandeur, but in process of time it became subject to Assyria. On the fall of Nineveh (B.C. 606) it threw off the Assyrian yoke, and became the capital of the growing Babylonian empire. **Under Nebuchadnezzar it became one of the most splendid cities of the ancient world.** After passing through various vicissitudes the city was occupied by Cyrus, "king of Elam," B.C. 538, who issued a decree permitting the Jews to return to their own land (Ezra 1). It then ceased to be the capital of an empire. It was again and again visited by hostile armies, till its inhabitants were all driven from their homes, and the city became a complete desolation, its very site being forgotten from among men. On the west bank of the Euphrates, about 50 miles south of Bagdad, there is found a series of artificial mounds of vast extent. These are the ruins of this once famous proud city. These ruins are principally (1) the great mound called Babil by the Arabs. This was probably the noted Temple of Belus, which was a pyramid about 480 feet high. (2) The Kasr (i.e., "the palace"). This was the great palace of Nebuchadnezzar. It is almost a square, each side of which is about 700 feet long. The little town of Hillah, near the site of Babylon, is built almost wholly of bricks taken from this single mound. (3) A lofty mound, on the summit of which stands a modern tomb called Amran ibn-Ali. This is probably the most ancient portion of the remains of the city, and represents the ruins of the famous hanging-gardens, or perhaps of some royal palace. The utter desolation of the city once called **"The**

glory of kingdoms" (Isa.13:19) was foretold by the prophets (Isa.13:4-22; Jer. 25:12; 50:2, 3; Dan. 2:31-38). The Babylon mentioned in 1 Pet. 5:13 was not Rome, as some have thought, but the literal city of Babylon, which was inhabited by many Jews at the time Peter wrote. **In Rev. 14:8; 16:19; 17:5; and 18:2, "Babylon" is supposed to mean Rome, not considered as pagan, but as the prolongation of the ancient power in the papal form. Rome, pagan and papal, is regarded as one power. "The literal Babylon was the beginner and supporter of tyranny and idolatry...This city and its whole empire were taken by the Persians under Cyrus; the Persians were subdued by the Macedonians, and the Macedonians by the Romans; so that Rome succeeded to the power of old Babylon. And it was her method to adopt the worship of the false deities she had conquered; so that by her own act she became the heiress and successor of all the Babylonian idolatry, and of all that was introduced into it by the immediate successors of Babylon, and consequently of all the idolatry of the earth. "Rome, or "mystical Babylon," is "that great city which reigneth over the kings of the earth" (17:18).**

Smith's Bible Dictionary

Bab'ylon in the Apocalypse, is the **symbolical name by which Rome is denoted. Revelation 14:8; Revelation 17:18**; The power of Rome was regarded by the later Jews as was that of

Babylon by their forefathers. Comp. Jeremiah 51:7; with Rev. 14:8 The occurrence of this name in 1Pe 5:13; has given rise to a variety of conjectures, many giving it the same meaning as in the Apocalypse; others refer it to Babylon in Asia, and others still to Babylon in Egypt. The most natural supposition of all is that by Babylon is intended the old Babylon of Assyria, which was largely inhabited by Jews at the time in question.

Gesenius's Lexicon

Babylon, a very ancient and celebrated city of Asia, the metropolis of Babylonia, Gen. 10:10; 2 Ki. 17:24; 20:12; Mic. 4:10, etc...The name of the city was applied to the province of Babylonia, Ps. 87:4; 137:1; Isa. 14:4, whence there is often mentioned "the king of Babylonia;" a name also given to the kings of Persia, as to Cyrus, Ezr. 5:13; to Artaxerxes, Neh. 13:6.

Conclusion

I would like to conclude by giving a prelude to the third and last title in this three part series on *The Revelation of John.* As was already pointed out above, the *Abomination of Desolation* has been reigning for over two thousand years and is soon to be judged and destroyed by the Man of Sin / Son of Perdition / antichrist. How this being arrives and when is the subject of the final title - *The Coming War in Heaven.* It has been my hope that by dividing *The Revelation of John* into three titles, the overall picture would be easier to comprehend.

CPSIA information can be obtained at www.ICGtesting.com
Printed in the USA
LVOW01s1335220715

447203LV00024B/413/P